GUSTAV HOLST

T0084194

SECOND SUITE IN F

FOR MILITARY BAND (1911)

Op.28 No.2
H.106

Revised Full Score based on the
autograph manuscript

Edited by Colin Matthews

Q.M.B. 502

BOOSEY & HAWKES

AN IMAGEM COMPANY

DISTRIBUTED BY

HAL•LEONARD®
CORPORATION
7777 W. BLUEMOUND RD. P.O. BOX 13819 MILWAUKEE, WI 53213

INTRODUCTION

Like the *First Suite* of 1909, the *Second Suite* for military band had to wait more than ten years before it entered the repertoire. Composed in 1911, it did not receive a public performance until June 30th 1922, when the band of the Royal Military School of Music, Kneller Hall, played it at the Royal Albert Hall, London. The programme note for that performance stated that the Suite had been 'put aside and forgotten' after 1911. Yet the manuscript (now in the British Library, London, Add. MS 47825) shows signs of considerable haste, and a great deal of revision*, and Imogen Holst believed that the work was originally written for a specific occasion (possibly the 1911 'Festival of Empire' held at the Crystal Palace), even if it was not performed at that time.

Unlike its predecessor, the *Second Suite* is based entirely on material from folk songs and morris dances. The scoring is more economical than in the *First Suite*, but in contrast to that work, Holst did not allow for any *ad lib* instruments**. Consequently the smallest band which can play the work as originally written would have to consist of 23 players plus percussion (as opposed to 19 for the *First Suite*). This revised edition differs from the original manuscript only in the addition of parts for bass clarinet and baritone and bass saxophones: these may be omitted at the conductor's discretion. It is of interest that Holst initially used only an alto saxophone; the tenor saxophone was a later addition, and for the most part takes over the part which had originally been intended for baritone (saxhorn), which Holst himself deleted.

Set out below is the original instrumentation, compared with that of the score first published in 1948. (The set of parts was first issued by Boosey & Co. in 1922; the 1948 full score incorporates additional instruments to make the work more suitable for American bands. As with the *First Suite*, the score was compiled from the parts without reference to the original manuscript.

 * The Finale 'Fantasia on the Dargason' is almost identical to the finale of the *St Paul's Suite* for string orchestra, composed in 1913. The manuscript of that work has many markings on it which relate to the *Second Suite*, and it seems clear that Holst must have made a revision at around the same time as he was composing the *St Paul's Suite*. To judge from the appearance of the manuscript, the first 23 pages of the finale (out of a total of 27) were rewritten. The most important change evident in the manuscript is, however, in the first movement, which originally had an entirely different opening. It also seems likely that the third movement was either rewritten or even added to the work at a later date.

 ** There are, however, cues in the second movement, where Holst's intentions are far from clear.

Manuscript	1948 Score
Flute/Piccolo in D♭	C Flute & Piccolo
E♭ Clarinet	Oboe
Oboe	E♭ Clarinet
Solo & 1st Clarinet in B♭	Solo B♭ Clarinet
2nd Clarinet in B♭	1st B♭ Clarinet
3rd Clarinet in B♭	2nd B♭ Clarinet
E♭ (Alto) Saxophone	3rd B♭ Clarinet
B♭ (Tenor) Saxophone	B♭ Bass Clarinet
2 Bassoons	1st Bassoon
	2nd Bassoon
Solo & 1st Cornets in B♭	E♭ Alto Saxophone
2nd Cornet in B♭	B♭ Tenor Saxophone
4 Horns in E♭ & F	E♭ Baritone Saxophone
2 Tenor Trombones	B♭ Bass Saxophone
1 Bass Trombone	Solo & 1st B♭ Cornet
Euphonium	2nd B♭ Cornet
Basses	4 Horns in F
Side Drum	2 Tenor Trombones
Bass Drum	Bass Trombone
Cymbals	Euphonium
Triangle	Basses
Tambourine	
Anvil	Drums (as manuscript)

In this revised edition, the alto clarinet, contrabass clarinet, soprano saxophone and trumpets have been omitted. Bass clarinet, baritone saxophone and bass saxophone have been retained, but may be omitted if so desired. In the 1948 score, the baritone and bass saxophones (and contrabass clarinet) were made to double the bass brasses throughout; this has been taken out, and they are used only as a bass to the winds, and in tuttis. They should be omitted entirely from the second movement.

Indeed, although it is not the place of this score to recommend any particular performance practice, it is suggested that the second movement will benefit from the use of solo instruments; and that there is no need for more than 22 players to be used. It is not clear from the manuscript whether Holst intended the solo at the beginning of that movement to be played by oboe or clarinet, or both. This score follows what appears to have been Holst's first thought – a clarinet solo, with the oboe not joining the melody until bar 11.

At the beginning of the finale, Holst's original intention was for the alto saxophone to play alone. When he came to add the tenor saxophone part he doubled the melody, perhaps as a precaution. The conductor may here decide whether or not to revert to the original. It is also up to the conductor, depending upon the size of the band, to specify where the piccolo should play – since Holst did not divide the flute and piccolo parts. (It should certainly not play in the second movement.) The division between solo and 1st clarinet was not carried through by Holst, and although it has been retained in this score, there are nowhere more than three separate clarinet parts.

Colin Matthews
London 1984

INSTRUMENTATION

C Flute & Piccolo
Oboe
E♭ Clarinet
Solo & 1st B♭ Clarinet
2nd B♭ Clarinet
3rd B♭ Clarinet
Bass Clarinet (*ad lib*)
2 Bassoons

Alto Saxophone
Tenor Saxophone
Baritone Saxophone (*ad lib*)
Bass Saxophone (*ad lib*)

Solo & 1st B♭ Cornet
2nd B♭ Cornet
4 Horns in F
2 Tenor Trombones
Bass Trombone
Euphonium
Basses

Percussion (3 players):
    Side Drum
    Bass Drum
    Cymbals
    Triangle
    Tambourine
    Anvil

Duration: c. 10½ minutes

The editor and publishers wish to acknowledge the invaluable assistance
received from Dr Fred Fennell during the preparation of this edition.

BOOSEY & HAWKES Q.M.B. EDITION No.502

dedicated to James Causley Windram

SECOND SUITE IN F
for Military Band

GUSTAV HOLST
Op.28, No.2
revised and edited by
COLIN MATTHEWS

1. MARCH

Morris Dance

A
B
C Fl. & Picc.
Ob.
E♭ Cl.
Solo & 1st B♭ Cl.
2nd B♭ Cl.
3rd B♭ Cl.
B♭ Bass Cl.
Bsn.
a2
E♭ Alto Sax.
B♭ Ten. Sax.
E♭ Bar. Sax.
B♭ Bass Sax.
1st B♭ Cort.
2nd B♭ Cort.
1st & 2nd
Hn. in F
3rd & 4th
1st Tbne.
2nd Tbne.
3rd Tbne.
Euph.
Basses
S.D.
Perc.
Bass Drum
Cymbal
Triangle
f
p

D
C Fl. & Picc.
Ob.
E♭ Cl.
Solo & 1st B♭ Cl.
2nd B♭ Cl.
3rd B♭ Cl.
B♭ Bass Cl.
Bsn.
a2
E♭ Alto Sax.
B♭ Ten. Sax.
E♭ Bar. Sax.
B♭ Bass Sax.
D
1st B♭ Cort.
2nd B♭ Cort.
1st & 2nd
Hn. in F
3rd & 4th
1st Tbne.
2nd Tbne.
3rd Tbne.
Euph.
Basses
S.D.
Perc.
B.D.
Cym.
f

E *Swansea Town*

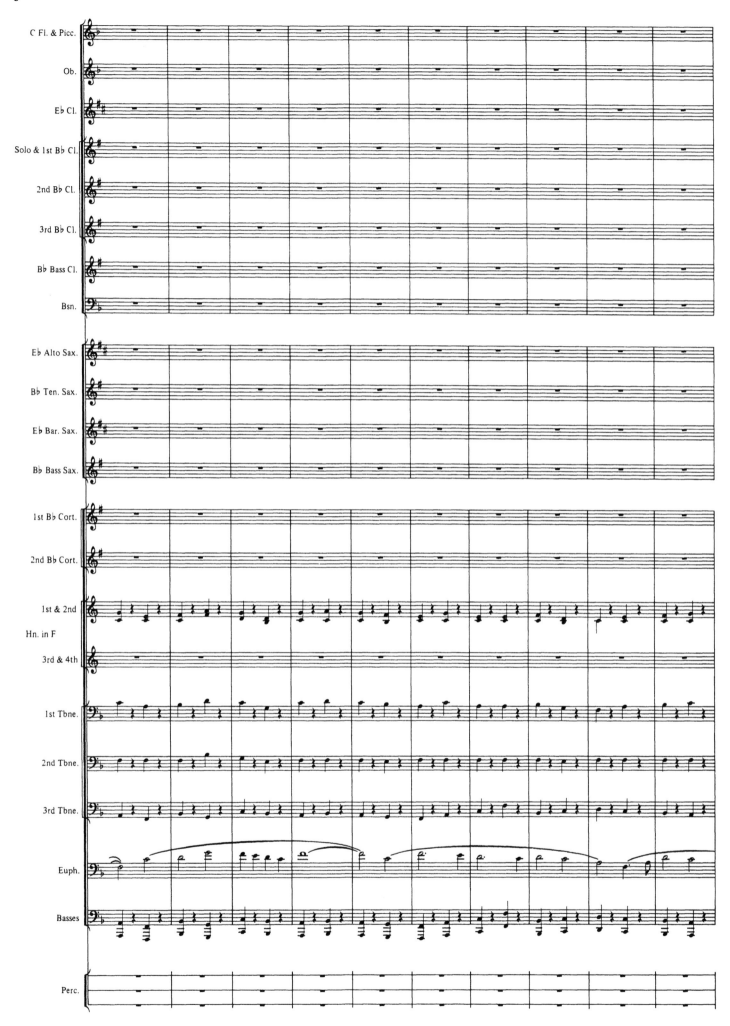

FINE

𝅗𝅥 = 𝅗𝅥. **H** *Claudy Banks*

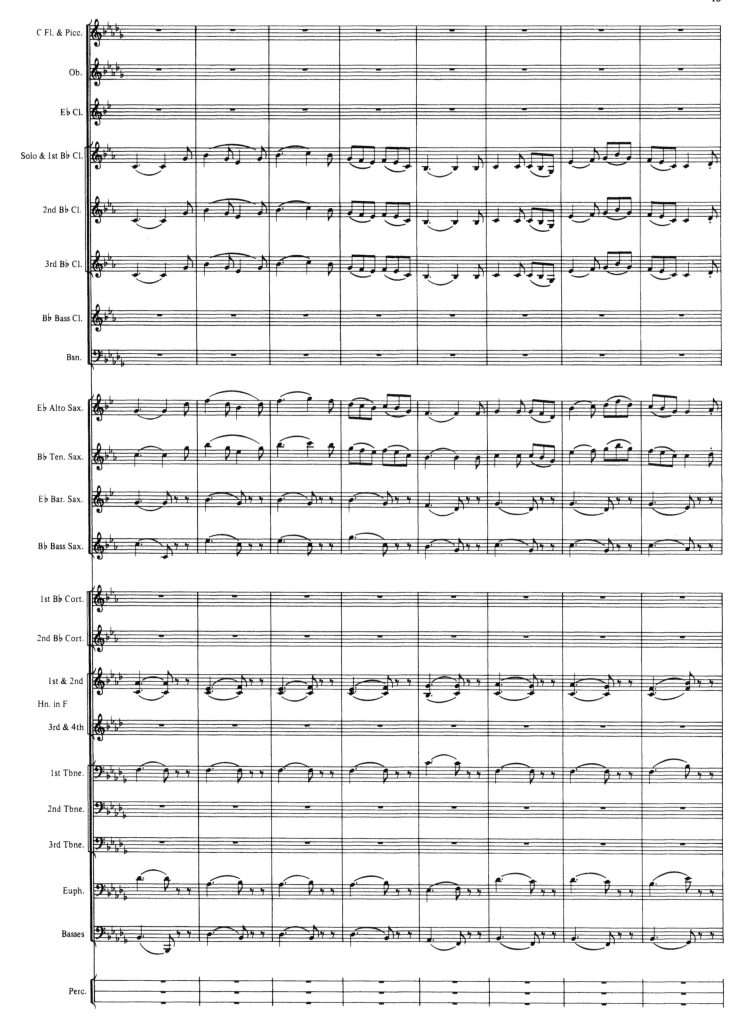

14

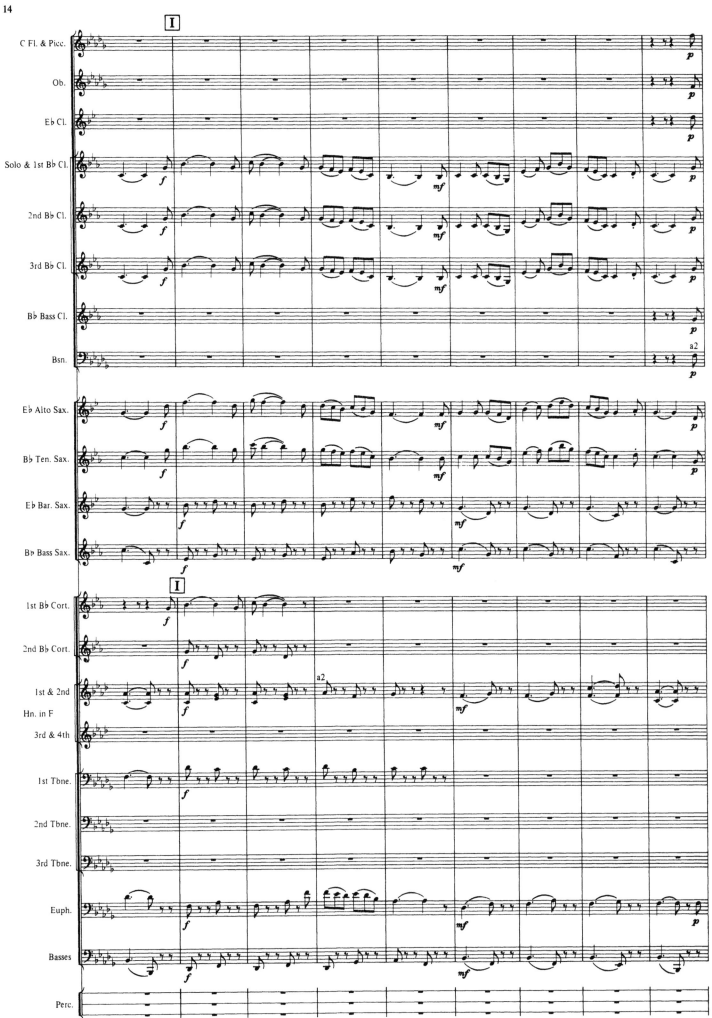

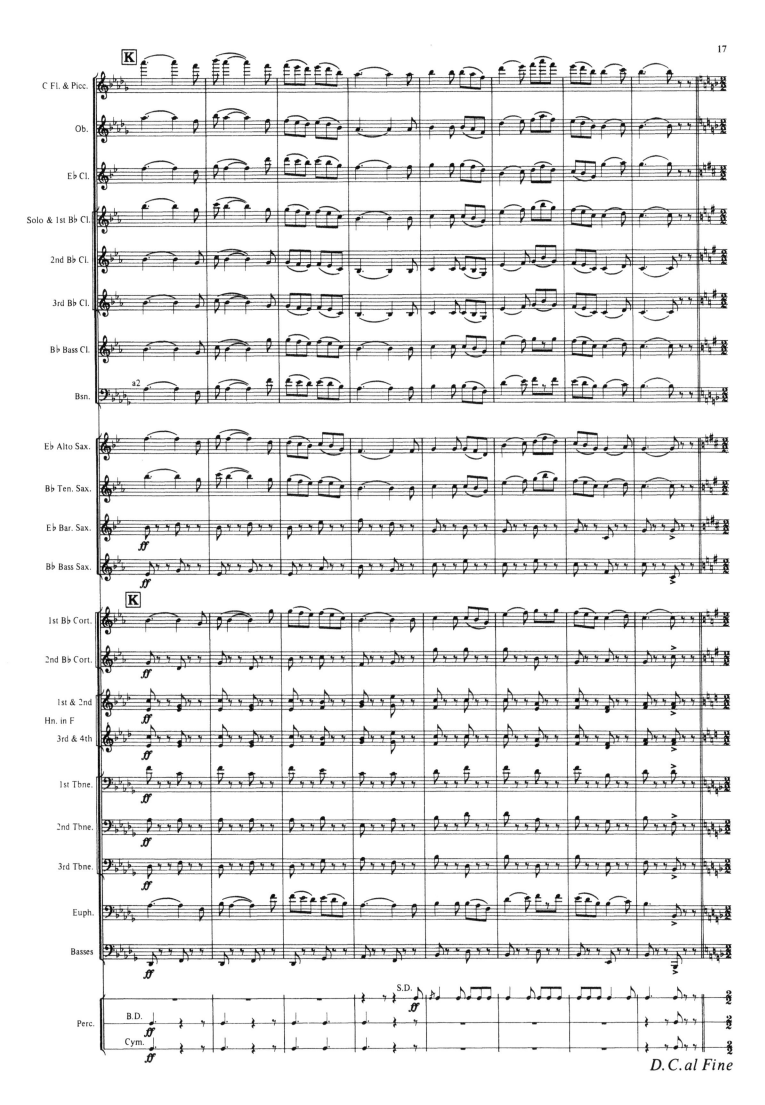

D.C. al Fine

2. SONG WITHOUT WORDS

'I'll love my love'

* See Introduction

3. SONG OF THE BLACKSMITH

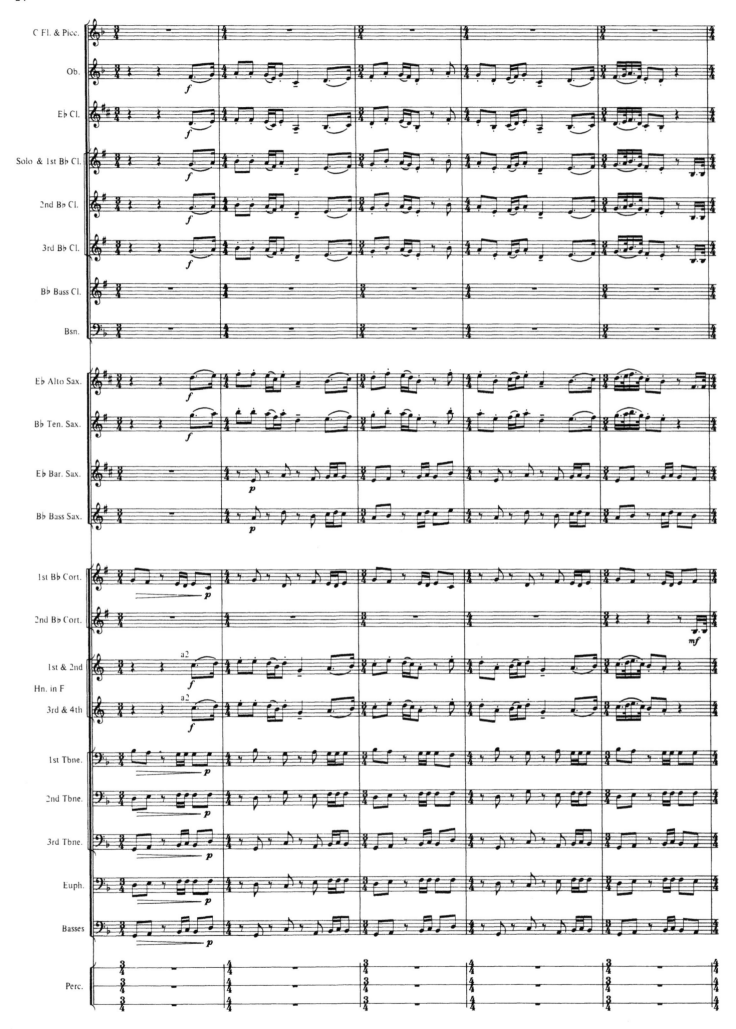

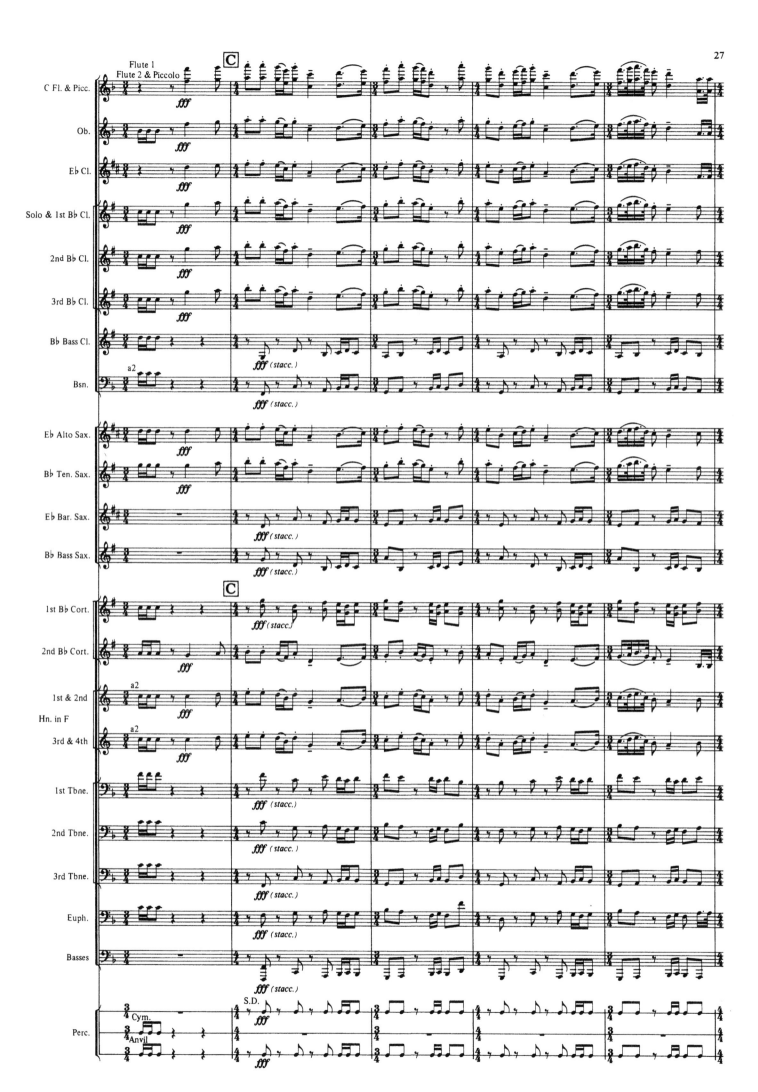

4. FANTASIA ON THE 'DARGASON'

* See Introduction

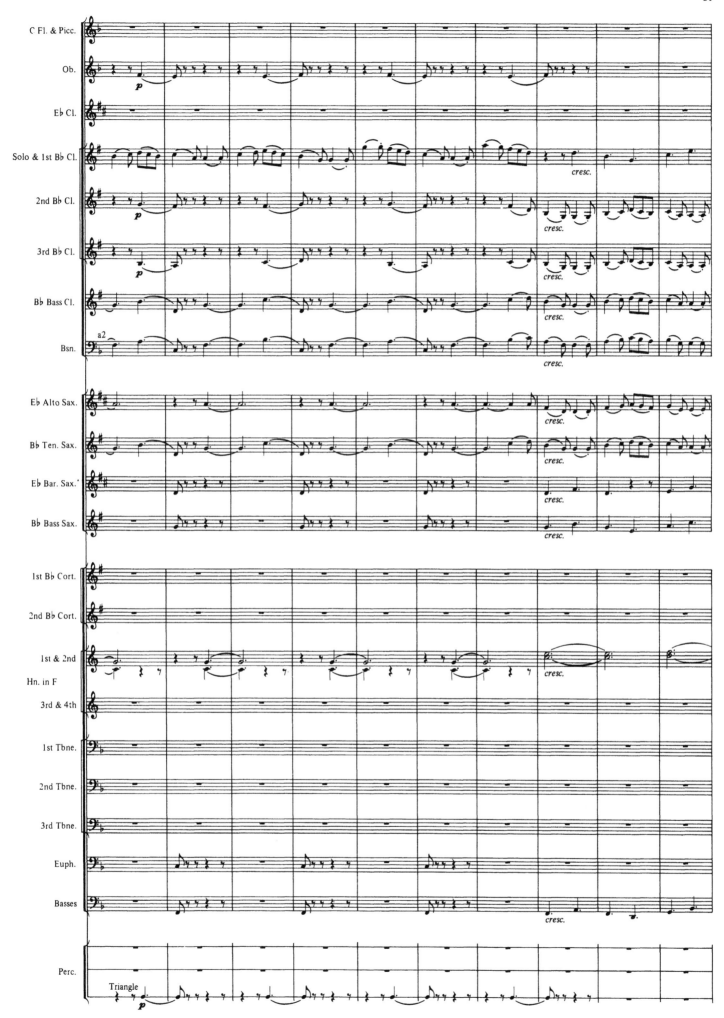

COLIN MATTHEWS

Colin Matthews was born in London in 1946. He read classics at the University of Nottingham, and then studied composition there with Arnold Whittall, and with Nicholas Maw. A number of works from the early 1970s won awards and prizes, but for several years his activities were as much musicological as compositional. Most notable was a collaboration with Deryck Cooke on the performing version of Mahler's Tenth Symphony, which began as early as 1964 and continued for more than a decade. In the last years of Benjamin Britten's life he worked closely with the composer, assisting him with his final compositions. Since 1972 he worked with the late Imogen Holst on the collected edition of her father's music. He was awarded the degree of Doctor of Philosophy for his work on Mahler by the University of Sussex, where for a time he taught composition and orchestration.

A Scottish National Orchestra award for his FOURTH SONATA brought Matthews wide recognition as a composer. Numerous commissions followed, and his NIGHT MUSIC for chamber orchestra, RAINBOW STUDIES, FIRST STRING QUARTET and DIVERTIMENTO for double string quartet have won international acclaim. More recently, his SONATA NO.5 'LANDSCAPE' (1983) has been premiered in London (BBC SO) and Berlin (Radio SO), and his CELLO CONCERTO was given at the BBC Promenade Concerts in 1984.

Biographical notes by courtesy of Faber Music Ltd., London

M-060-05256-9

HL48010590

ISBN 978-1-4768-9971-8